GERSHWIN®
ON
BROADWAY
(from 1919 to 1933)

CONTENTS

F O R E W O R D

This volume is the largest compilation of Gershwin songs ever published. It is made up of 89 songs that George Gershwin wrote for reviews and book shows that opened on Broadway between 1919 and 1933. They cover his career as an interpolator of material for productions written primarily by others, through to his last complete show score. Many of these selections were never widely distributed, and some have not been in print for 60 years!

We, the editors, gathered every song that Gershwin wrote for the Broadway stage. When it was apparent that a complete volume of these songs would have been uncomfortably bulky and incredibly expensive, we began the task of picking the best and most interesting of these songs. We were guided by the numerous requests for Gershwin songs that have recently attained new popularity and prominence, such as "LITTLE JAZZ BIRD," "BOY WANTED," "ISN'T IT A PITY," and "INNOCENT INGENUE BABY." We also wanted to return to print such Gershwin classics as "I WAS SO YOUNG, (You Were So Beautiful)," "THE HALF OF IT, DEARIE, BLUES," "MY COUSIN IN MILWAUKEE," and "LORELEI." In order to include all of these songs, there are some notable omissions, the most significant being "SWANEE." Because this song has appeared in literally hundreds of folios, we thought that, in leaving out this song, we could include another of historical importance.

So, we have included "MISCHA, JASCHA, TOSCHA, SASCHA," a George and Ira Gershwin song written in 1922. The song was originally written by the Gershwins to be performed at parties of their friends and associates. It was first published in a limited-edition songbook in 1932. Even though it has appeared in a few folios since then, the song has not been widely available. Due to the increased interest in this song, it has been included so that many more can play it, sing it, and enjoy it the way the Gershwins and their friends did 60 years ago. Additional songs that Gershwin wrote for Broadway shows that are not included in this volume are listed at the end of this foreword.

Due to the historical nature of this book, it was also decided that, where possible, original music plates would be used for the rarer titles. Unfortunately, printing being what it was in the 20's, some of the plates from these years were not in the best condition. Over the years, we have made new plates of Gershwin songs for various other folios and projects, and these new plates are included (often with musical and lyric corrections). However, the reader will note that some of the music pages reproduced in this volume are of lesser quality than others. We trust that this will not be distracting to those who would play and sing these very special songs, and we assure you that the best copies available were reproduced for use in this book.

We hope that this book is enjoyable, enlightening, and a very special part of your musical and theatre library, just as Gershwin and his music are a special part of all of our lives.

Jeff Sultanof

Additional "GERSHWIN ON BROADWAY" Songs Available

Song Title	Broadway Show		Folio Number
Bride and Groom	"OH, KAY"	(Vocal Sel.)	SF0106
Dance Alone with You	"FUNNY FACE"	(Vocal Sel.)	SF0108
Dear Little Girl	"OH, KAY"	(Vocal Sel.)	SF0106
Don't Ask	"OH, KAY"	(Vocal Sel.)	SF0106
Hangin' Around with You	"STRIKE UP THE BAND"	(Vocal Sel.)	SF0093
Heaven on Earth	"OH, KAY"	(Vocal Sel.)	SF0106
The Illegitimate Daughter	"OF THEE I SING"	(Vocal Sel.)*	SF0139
I Mean to Say	"STRIKE UP THE BAND"	(Vocal Sel.)	SF0093
In the Swim	"MY ONE AND ONLY"	(Vocal Sel.)	VF1055
I Want to Be a War Bride	"STRIKE UP THE BAND"	(Vocal Sel.)	SF0093
The Senator from Minnesota	"OF THEE I SING"	(Vocal Sel.)*	SF0139
Show Me the Town	"OH, KAY"	(Vocal Sel.)	SF0106
The Woman's Touch	"OH, KAY"	(Vocal Sel.)	SF0106
The World Is Mine	"FUNNY FACE"	(Vocal Sel.)	SF0108

*Complete Vocal Score also Available – VP0012

GEORGE GERSHWIN BIOGRAPHY

George Gershwin was born in Brooklyn, New York on September 26, 1898. He was the second of four children born to Morris and Rose Gershwin, who came to the United States from Russia.

Gershwin grew up on New York's lower East Side. In 1912, he began studying piano with Charles Hambitzer, noted pianist and composer. It was Hambitzer who introduced him to the classic piano literature and exposed him to the modern concert music of the time. Gershwin later said that Hambitzer made him "harmony conscious."

In May 1916, Gershwin quit school to become a song demonstrator (or "plugger") for the Remick Music Publishing Company. He soon established himself as one of the best pianists in the song publishing business and began making piano rolls.

In 1917, he joined the Harms Publishing Company as a staff composer. Max Dreyfus, who ran the company, was immediately impressed by Gershwin's talent. (He later encouraged and gave similar contracts to Rodgers and Hart, Cole Porter, and Vincent Youmans.) Gershwin's fame and confidence grew with his first hit, "SWANEE," and his first full Broadway score "LA, LA LUCILLE," both written in 1919.

During the 20's, Gershwin wrote songs for shows and revues, and in 1922, wrote his second concert work, a 20 minute opera, "BLUE MONDAY," for the "GEORGE WHITE'S SCANDALS OF 1922." Unfortunately, it was removed from the show after opening night. However, Gershwin and Paul Whiteman, the Scandals' conductor, struck up a friendship. Whiteman promised to commission a work from Gershwin for a jazz concert that he would one day give. That day came on February 12, 1924, when "A RHAPSODY IN BLUE" created a sensation at Aeolian Hall in Paul Whiteman's

first "EXPERIMENT IN MODERN MUSIC." The "RHAPSO has since become the most frequently performed con composition by an American composer, and Gershw most popular piece.

Many of Gershwin's greatest songs date from the 1920's, among them "THE MAN I LOVE", "SOMEONE WATCH OVER ME", "'S WONDERFUL" and "HE LOVES A SHE LOVES." On December 3, 1925, Gershwin was soloist in his own piano concerto, "CONCERTO IN F" c missioned by the New York Symphony. He premiered "THREE PRELUDES" for piano on December 4, 1926, his tone-poem "AN AMERICAN IN PARIS " was first pla by Walter Damrosch and The New York Philharmonic December 13, 1928. All of these works have become sta in the concert literature and continue to grow in popul around the world.

The '30s brought Gershwin more acclaim in the the ("STRIKE UP THE BAND," "GIRL CRAZY," "OF THEE I SIN and in the concert hall. "CUBAN OVERTURE" (1932) ar GOT RHYTHM VARIATIONS" (1934) gave evidence to (shwin's growing mastery of counterpoint and orches tion, which culminated in the opera "PORGY AND BE Many historians believe "PORGY AND BESS" not onl be Gershwin's masterpiece, but the best opera compo by an American; indeed, one of the finest written in 20th Century.

Gershwin moved to Hollywood in 1936 and the so "THEY CAN'T TAKE THAT AWAY FROM ME," "A FOGGY D "LET'S CALL THE WHOLE THING OFF," and "THEY LAUGHED" date from that period. Gershwin suddenly came ill in July 1937. A brain tumor was diagnosed surgery was performed on July 11. Portions were remo but the composer never regained consciousness. He c that same day.

I WAS SO YOUNG
(You Were So Beautiful)

Words By
IRVING CAESAR and ALFRED BRYAN

Music By
GEORGE GERSHWIN

You were a girl with a wo - man's art,___
Hearts that are young find a love that's new,___

And you held my fate in your hand. _____
When they wake from fool - ish dreams. _____

I was the moth___   You were the flame,___
Poor lit - tle moth___   Chas - ing the flame,___

Ped.   *   Ped.   *

SOME WONDERFUL SORT OF SOMEONE

Words By
SCHUYLER GREENE

Music By
GEORGE GERSHWIN

-bue each of you with a whole lot of pa-tience and a mod-est share of love
sly lit-tle, shy lit-tle, spry lit-tle fel-low with an ar-row and a bow

Sure-ly as the lit-tle stars are up a - bove.
Had his eye up - on you and be - fore you know.

Refrain.

Some won-der-ful sort of some-one, Some morn - ing, ____

____ with - out warn - ing _____ will hap - pen a-

-long_____ And some day, some won-der-ful sort of some-one will bring you _____ joy and sing you _____ one won-der-ful song _____ And when for you life takes on a new charm and all the fu-ture seems ro - sy, There in a cot-tage

THE BEST OF EVERYTHING

Words By
B.G. DeSYLVA and ARTHUR JACKSON

Music by
GEORGE GERSHWIN

noon. _____ That my pa - rents had a
-nied. _____ For the clothes I could af -

win - ner they knew right a - way; _____ For
-ford were scarce - ly wear - a - ble; _____ And

in my mouth they found a sil - ver spoon. _____ My
sub-ways were a wal - lop to my pride. _____ I

proud and lov - ing au - thors gave me all I could re -
had a cham - pagne ap - pe - tite but this was ver - y

- quest: My milk was al - ways cer - ti - fied; My
clear: My in - come, as the say - ing goes, Could

car - riage was the best, And from then up to the
on - ly pay for beer, I've been long - ing for the

pres - ent I've lived like a king; ———— And
day when I can have my fling; ———— And

al - ways had the best of ev - 'ry - thing. ————
al - ways have the best of ev - 'ry - thing. ————

Chorus

I get my rings and things from Tif-fan-y. I go to
I'd like my sa-bles from Re-vil-lon Freres. And Quel-ques

Ben - son - Hed - ges for cig - ar - ettes. _____
Fleurs' the scent that I love the best. _____

I al - ways wear Mc Cal - lum hos - ier - y_____ I go to
I wish Tap - pe could make the hats I wear_____ I'd like the

Budd for my_____ cra-vats Stet - son makes_____ my hats A
Ritz for ev - 'ry meal Gowns made by_____ Lu - cille And

LIMEHOUSE NIGHTS

Words By
B.G. DeSYLVA and JOHN HENRY MEARS

Music By
GEORGE GERSHWIN

Lon-don town is full of won-der-ful sights

Charm-ing days and dark mys-ter-i-ous nights

But in the

Lon - don slums, ___ Just as the twi - light comes ___

There is a cap - ti - va - ting ren - dez - vous ___

It is known as Lime - house

ev - e - ry-where ___ Dream - ers go

to seek for - get - ful-ness there _____

Its wom - en quick-ly fade __ its worth-less men have made __

Lime - house Nights, Won - der - ful the whole world through. _____

Refrain

Lime _____ house Nights _____

THE LOVE OF A WIFE

Words By
B.G. DeSYLVA and ARTHUR JACKSON

Music By
GEORGE GERSHWI

lend an ear; So we can make the mat - ter clear: In

case you con - tem - plate ____ The ma - tri - mon - i - al state.

Refrain

Oh, the love of a wife ____ is a won-der-ful thing. ____

____ Take it from us, take it from us: We're sure! ____

Wives are much bet - ter for us Than the girls from the chor - us Or the love of a sweet man - i - cure. All the hugs and all the Kis - ses That a fel - low gets from his mis - sus Are the

kind that nev - er fill him with re - grets._____ Oh, the

love of a wife _____ is a won - der - ful thing _____

_ But it's some - thing that a hus - band nev - er

1 gets.

2 Oh, the gets._____

NOBODY BUT YOU

Words By
ARTHUR JACKSON and B.G. DeSYLVA

Music By
GEORGE GERSHW

Refrain

POPPYLAND

Words By
B.G. DeSYLVA and JOHN HENRY MEARS

Music By
GEORGE GERSHWIN

a dream of col-or-ful de-light, Each bud is

bloom-ing for you. So come with

poco rit.

rall. *poco rit.*

Refrain

me where the blos-soms grow in Pop-py-land

— What joy 'Twill be just we two dear, stroll-ing hand in

hand _____ We'll hear the drow-sy hum of the bees,

p subit

Borne up-on the whis-per-ing breeze, There I'll tell that

won-der-ful sto-ry, and you'll un-der-stand, For lurk-ing

deep in the heart of each se-duc-tive flow'r _____ That gai-ly

WE'RE PALS

Words By
IRVING CAESAR

Music By
GEORGE GERSHWIN

me, If you could on - ly speak; _____ I

want to tell you I feel, That our friendship is real: We're

Refrain (*Slow with great exspression*)

pals, a cou-ple of pals, A cou-ple of

true pals, that's what we are, _____ We've been

through thick and thin, Both trav-el-ing side by side

far and wide, Land or sea, there were we, Most times

we'd no place to go, But I nev-er wor-ried

with you a - long,_____ Though there is no way that I can

MY LADY

Words By
ARTHUR JACKSON

Music By
GEORGE GERSHWIN

BOY WANTED

Music and Lyrics by
GEORGE GERSHWIN
and ARTHUR FRANCIS

I LOVE YOU

Words By
ARTHUR JACKSON

Music By
GEORGE GERSHWIN

I don't speak the lan - guag - es, I don't e - ven try,

I just say "I love you, dear," And that gets me by.

Refrain

I love you, _____ I love

you, _____ When two hearts beat "pit - ter - pat-

- - ter," What does the lan - guage mat - ter? I

want you, _____ To love me, too, _____

Words don't wor - ry me, dear, I need on - ly three, dear,

I love you. _____ you. _____

DANCING SHOES

Music and Lyrics by
GEORGE GERSHWIN
and ARTHUR FRANCIS

make you treas-ure ev-'ry meas-ure Of a rag-gy

strain; Danc-ing shoes bring a glad-ness and a mad-ness

That go to your brain

They will make you frol - ic, Lose the di - a - bol - ic,

Wea - ry mel - an - chol - ic blues.

If the world's "a - gin" you, Show there's some - thing in you,

Try a pair of danc - ing shoes, And

Refrain

you'll start to sway in a gay sort of

way; In a trance, you'll dance and lose the dog - gone blues—

Oh! boy! then joy fills the air, not a care, a-ny-where, For there's mag-ic in a pair of danc-ing shoes.

SOME RAIN MUST FALL

Music and Lyrics by
GEORGE GERSHWIN
and IRA GERSHWIN

Old - er, wis - er, now, I plain - ly see.

Refrain

p-f

Some rain must fall, _____ For

one and all, _____ Send - ing all our

dreams a - stray, They fly a - way, _____ When skies are

SOUTH SEA ISLES

Words By
ARTHUR JACKSON

Music By
GEORGE GERSHWIN

A mys-tic land, That tells a sto-ry, On ev-'ry hand,
The sav-age chants, As night ad-vanc-es The wild ro-mance

Of trop-ic glor-y, Here, _____ care and wor-ries dis-ap-
Of sav-age danc-es All _____ seem to lure me with their

-pear; _____ And ev-'ry-where, The flowers blooming,
call. _____ The reck-less love, That sets you reel-ing,

With fra-grance rare, The air per-fum-ing, Here
That soars a-bove All oth-er feel-ing, All

— Par-a-dise is ver-y near. ———— I love those
— seem to hold me in their thrall. ———— I love those

Refrain

Sun-ny South Sea Is-lands,— Gold-en trop-ic

sky — lands, Land of palms and bright-col-ored birds,—

ACROSS THE SEA

Words By
B.G. DeSYLVA and E. RAY GOETZ

Music By
GEORGE GERSHWIN

there, Oh, girl of my dreams you come from out the sea I know, At

twi-light it seems I hear you call-ing me, and so: My

Refrain (*Con Expressione*)

heart will sail a - cross the sea in search of

you; _____ In a frag - ile dream _____ boat,

of a love - ly hue, _____ Un - til the Vis - ion

that I see in dreams come true _____ My

heart will sail a - cross the sea in search __ of __

you.   My   you. _____

CINDERELATIVES

Words By
B.G. DeSYLVA and E. RAY GOETZ

Music By
GEORGE GERSHWIN

My days of child-hood glor - y, With fai - ry-tales were blest, ——— The Cin-der-el - la sto - ry, I al-ways liked the best, ———

But those gold - en days are gone; And in-stead, I seek the foot - lights glare, And lit - tle Cin - der - el - la, Still lives · to haunt me there.

Refrain

All the dain-ty dar-lings of ___ The plays I love In sweet-ness ex - ceed; ___ But they all owe a kiss to Cin-der - el - la, ___ For they fol - low ___ her lead, That is, they start in rags; But

I'LL BUILD A STAIRWAY TO PARADISE

Words By
B.G. DeSYLVA and IRA GERSHWIN

Music By
GEORGE GERSHWIN

INNOCENT INGENUE BABY

Words By
BRIAN HOOKER

Music By
WILLIAM DALY and GEORGE GERSHWIN

-rene. I don't wish to trou-ble you
-dise? Though I seem in-quis-i-tive,

For a "Yes" or "No;" Still, if you see___ what I
Tell me, I im-plore, Are you a vamp___ in dis-

mean, It's quite dis-tress-ing___ To won-der so.
-guise? A mere flir-ta-tion?___ Or some-thing more?

Refrain *(Delicately)*

p-f

In-no-cent In-ge-nue Ba-by Say, if I fell for you, ba-by,

Would you not love me true, ba - by, true? _____

Flap - pers are not so few, ba - by, E - qual - ly fair to

view, ba - by — Wil - ling to bill and coo, ba - by, too!

But there's a some-thing, some-where, some - how, smil - ing in your

WALKING HOME WITH ANGELINE

Words By
BRIAN HOOKER

Music By
GEORGE GERSHWIN

Down by the school-house gate, To - night at eight,
Still, as the sun - set smiles for miles and miles,

Af - ter the sing - in' school is through
Still, in the moon-light cool and blue

old Town Clock is strik - ing nine,_____ And the
gets as late as half - past nine,_____ And the

clouds are bright e - nough to see their col - or by,_____ And the
skies are soft - ly beam - ing, And the fun - ny moon_____ Some-how

Kat - y - dids and crick - ets sing their lul - la - by;_____ There's a
seem-ing to be dream-ing of a hon - ey - moon,_____ And the

feel - ing in this heart of mine,_____ Like a
lit - tle stars come out and shine,_____ And the

SHE HANGS OUT IN OUR ALLEY

Words By
B.G. DeSYLVA and E. RAY GOETZ

Music By
GEORGE GERSHWIN

Allegro

Ev-'ry Mon - day morn at the break of dawn When the sun is up and the milk-man's gone I ser - e - nade a husk - y maid, From the Al - ley flat where I park my hat I can

watch her work and I figure that I'd like to
see her work for me, She
weighs in at three hun-dred three I wish it all be-longed to me!

Refrain

She hangs out in our Al-ley, She's pal-ly, like Sal-ly, Her

THERE IS NOTHING TOO GOOD FOR YOU

Words By
B.G. DeSYLVA and E. RAY GOETZ

Music By
GEORGE GERSHWIN

LET'S BE LONESOME TOGETHER

Words By
B.G. DeSYLVA and E. RAY GOETZ

Music By
GEORGE GERSHWIN

Has ruin-ed my high 'C'; You look so hap-py-
'Cause I'm a-lone and blue And let me say it's

is-n't it queer —— I'm lone-some as can be". —— The
eas-y to see That you are lone-ly, too —— So,

gold-fish said: "You're wrong, my dear, I'm lone some too".
as the fair ca-na-ry did I'd like to do;

Then I heard the fair ca-na-ry coo: ——
Let me share my lone-li-ness with you. ——

poco rit

Refrain
(*Slow and liltingly*)

"Let's be lone-some to-geth — er,

Why be lone-some a-lone? — Two to-

-geth-er can weath — er A — ny

weath-er that's known; — We'll soon

re - a - lize _____ Lone - li - ness can be a bless - ing

in dis - guise; _____ So let's be lone-some to-geth-

- er _ Then we won't be lone-some at all." _

YOU AND I
(In Old Versailles)

Words By
B.G. DeSYLVA

Music By
GEORGE GERSHWIN and JACK GREEN

find me Sing-ing, as the night shad-ows fall: _____

Refrain *(not fast)*

"You and I _____ one day in old Ver-sailles Said good-by _____ _____ as the day was fad - ing. When the dawn _____ was gray-ing, old Ver-sailles _____ you had gone, _____ And my heart had, too. _____

But now it seems _____ In my twi - light dreams _____

___ I see you there _____ By the foun-tains play - ing, say - ing;

'Don't you cry; ___ For I'm re - turn - ing to Old Ver-sailles, ___

___ Love o'mine, and you!'" _____ you!'" _____

THE HALF OF IT, DEARIE, BLUES

Music and Lyrics by
GEORGE GERSHWIN
and IRA GERSHWIN

(He) Each time you trill a song with Bill, or look at Will, I get a chill— I'm
(She) You dare as-sert that you were hurt each time I'd flirt with Bill or Bert— You

gloom - y.   I won't re-call the names of all the men who fall— it's all ap-
brute, you!   Well I'm re-paid; I felt be-trayed when an - y maid whom you sur-

-pal - ling to me.   Of course I real - ly can-not blame them a bit,—
-veyed would suit you.   Com-pared to you, I've been as good as could be—

For you're a hit,— wher-e'er you flit.— I know it's so, but dear-ie,
Yet here you are,— lec-tur-ing me!— You're just a guy who makes me

oh! you'll nev-er know the blues that go Right through me.
cry, yet though I try to "cut" you I Sa-lute you.

poco rit.

Refrain *smoothly*

I've got the "You don't know the half of it, dear-ie," blues!—
I've got the "You don't know the half of it, dear-ie," blues!—

The troub-le is you have so
Oh, how I wish you'd drop an

man-y from whom to choose._____
an-chor and end your cruise._____

If you should mar-ry Tom, Dick or Har-ry, Life would be— the bunk-
You're just a duf-fer Who makes me suf-fer; All the young-er set

I'd be-come a monk. I've got the "You don't know the half of it, dear-ie," blues!
Says your heart's to let. I've got the "You don't know the half of it, dear-ie," blues!

THE JIJIBO

Words By
B.G. DeSYLVA

Music By
GEORGE GERSHWIN

I bought a lit-tle book by chance,— "How to get Fat or Thin."—

What do you think I read?— What do you think it said?—

It told a-bout a cer-tain dance— Bad for your doub-le-chin.— Right on

the peo - ple know — The "Ji - ji - bo" — is ap - ro - pos!

How can you miss? Paste it in your hat! First you shake this —

then you shake that! If you want a fig - ure that is slim and grace - ful

accel

This - 'll bring the thing a - bout; — Or if you need a ton - ic that - 'll

accel

make your face full, This is what-'ll puff you out!____ So,

ev-'ry-bod-y ought to know ____ the "Ji-ji-bo"____ The "Ji-ji-bo"____ is all the

go;— Fol-low the crowd and do the "Ji-ji-

1
-bo!"

2
-bo!"____

MAH-JONGG

Words By
B.G. DeSYLVA

Music By
GEORGE GERSHWIN

From the sly Chi - nee, man - y years B. C. Comes a leg - en - da - ry

song — Of a love - game played, for a charm - ing maid, Who

an - swered to the name, Mah Jongg — If cor - rect - ly sung, it will

Refrain *(sustained)*

Mah _____ Jongg _____
Mah _____ Jongg _____

Mah _____ Jongg! _____
Mah _____ Jongg! _____

Maid - en fair, When 'er I sing to thee, _____
Love - ly lit - tle Or - i - en - tal witch, _____

Thoughts of love ex - cite me and I go off the key. ____ Mah _____
In the box - es down at Ab - er - crom-bie and Fitch! Mah _____

SOMEONE BELIEVES IN YOU

Words By
B.G. DeSYLVA

Music By
GEORGE GERSHWIN

Slowly

When you're plod - ding on your wear - y way

It helps a lot to get a bit of

cheer, Like this note that

KONGO KATE

Words By
B.G. DeSYLVA

Music By
GEORGE GERSHWIN

In the land of Kon - go Where the gals are pips

There lives a la - dy known as Kate.

She can do a tan - go On - ly with her hips,

You'd love her she is dressed in on - ly a hat.—

Lots of this and plen - ty of that.— Kon - go Kate you tell 'em

Kon - go Kate,— None can com - pare to

you,— Oh, what a shoul - der she can wield,

SOMEBODY LOVES ME

Words By
B.G. DeSYLVA and BALLARD MacDONALD

Music By
GEORGE GERSHWIN

I NEED A GARDEN

Words By
B.G. DeSYLVA

Music By
GEORGE GERSHWIN

In such _____ sur - round - ings _____ I'd

coo like _____ a dove _____ For on - ly _____

— a gar - den _____ can help one _____ make

love. (So) love. _____

FASCINATING RHYTHM

Music and Lyrics by
GEORGE GERSHWIN
and IRA GERSHWIN

Moderato

Got a lit-tle rhy-thm, A rhy-thm, a rhy-thm That pit-a-pats through my brain. So darn per-sis-tent, The day is-n't dis-tant When it-'ll drive me in-sane. Comes in the morn-ing With-

out an-y warn-ing, And hangs a-round all day. I'll have to sneak up to it,

Some-day, and speak up to it, I hope it list-ens when I say:

REFRAIN

"Fas-ci-nat-ing Rhy-thm You've got me on the go! Fas-ci-nat-ing Rhy-thm I'm all a-

qui-ver. What a mess you're mak-ing! The neigh-bors want to know why I'm

Won't you take a day off? De - cide to run a-long Some-where far a-way off, And make it snap-py!

Oh, how I long to be __ the man I used to be!

Fas-ci- nat-ing Rhy-thm, Oh, won't you stop pick-ing on me!"

me!"

NIGHT TIME IN ARABY

Words By
B.G. DeSYLVA

Music By
GEORGE GERSHWIN

And there is them as calls it great.

There is not a dan - cer that this ba - by can - not beat, And she does - n't ev - en use her feet.

Refrain
Moderato assai

p-f

They call her Con - go Kate You'd love her Kon - go Kate,

You'd love her she is dressed in on-ly a hat.—

Lots of this and plen-ty of that.— Kon - go Kate you tell 'em

Kon - go Kate,——— None can com-pare to

you,——————— Oh, what a shoul-der she can wield,

SOMEBODY LOVES ME

Words By
B.G. DeSYLVA and BALLARD MacDONALD

Music By
GEORGE GERSHWIN

118

I NEED A GARDEN

Words By
B.G. DeSYLVA

Music By
GEORGE GERSHWIN

FASCINATING RHYTHM

Music and Lyrics by
GEORGE GERSHWIN
and IRA GERSHWIN

NIGHT TIME IN ARABY

Words By
B.G. DeSYLVA

Music By
GEORGE GERSHWIN

Refrain *(con expressione.)*

Night- time is fall-ing in Ar - a - by, ———————

My heart is call- ing for Ar - a - by,

I can hear, sweet and clear, O - ver the sea, ———

Some-one true, call-ing to me; ———————

LITTLE JAZZ BIRD

Music and Lyrics by
GEORGE GERSHWIN
and IRA GERSHWIN

In - to a cab-a-ret, one fa-tal day a lit-tle song-bird

flew; Found it so ve-ry gay, he thought he'd stay, Just to

get a bird's eye - view. When he heard the jazz-band play - ing, He was hap-py as a lark; To each mea - sure he kept sway - ing; And he stayed 'till af - ter dark,... Then back to the land he knew, thrilled through and through, He

HANG ON TO ME

Music and Lyrics by
GEORGE GERSHWIN
and IRA GERSHWIN

Moderato

Trou-ble may hound us, Shad-ow sur-round us, Nev-er mind, my dear.

Don't be down heart-ed, When we get start-ed, They will dis-ap - pear.

Lis-ten to broth-er, While we've each oth-er There's no need to fear,

For like Hän - sel and Gre-tel We will prove our met - tle.

Refrain *In very slow Fox-trot time*

If you hang on to me, While I hang on to you, We'll dance

in-to the sun-shine out of the rain.— (For ev-er and a day) Don't sigh

we'll get a-long; Just try hum-ming a song, And my! soon we will hear the

blue-bird a-gain.   That's right!   Hold tight!   We're on our way!

Up-hill   un-til   we lose the shad - ows.   If you

hang on to me,   While I   hang on to you,   We'll dance in-to the sun-shine

out of the rain.   out of the rain.

OH, LADY BE GOOD!

Music and Lyrics by
GEORGE GERSHWIN
and IRA GERSHWIN

Allegretto grazioso

Lis - ten to my tale of woe, It's ter - ri - bly sad, but true.
Au - burn and bru - nette and blonde, I love 'em all, tall or small.

All dressed up, no place to go, Each ev - 'ning I'm aw - f'ly blue.
But some - how they don't grow fond, They stag - ger but nev - er fall.

I must win some win - some miss; Can't go on like this.
Win - ter's gone, and now it's Spring! Love! where is thy sting?

THE MAN I LOVE

Music and Lyrics by
GEORGE GERSHWIN
and IRA GERSHWIN

When the mel-low moon be-gins to beam, Ev-'ry night I dream a lit-tle dream,

And of course Prince Charm-ing is the theme, The he for me. Al-

145

SO AM I

Music and Lyrics by
GEORGE GERSHWIN
and IRA GERSHWIN

148

MY FAIR LADY

Words By
B.G. DeSYLVA and IRA GERSHWIN

Music By
GEORGE GERSHWIN

THREE TIMES A DAY

Words By
B.G. DeSYLVA and IRA GERSHWIN

Music By
GEORGE GERSHWIN

Allegretto

Kenneth: If I had my way I'd trail you night and
Peggy: Yes I re - a - lize That you are ver - y

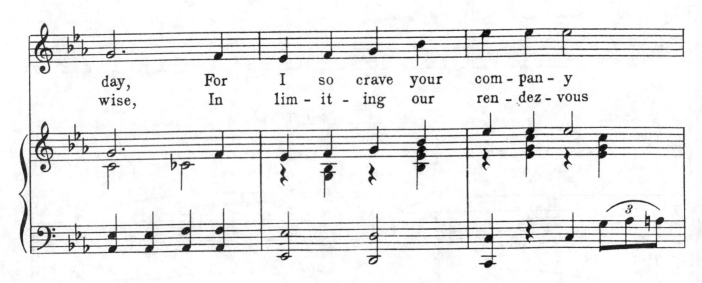

day, For I so crave your com - pan - y
wise, In lim - it - ing our ren - dez - vous

I'd be in it ev - 'ry min - ute! But, up - on my
Such a stand - 'll cause no scan - dal. Just three times a

soul, I'll ex - er - cise con - trol; In case it be that
day Is quite e - nough, I'd say; But if your calls are

you should see More than just e - nough of me!
more than three Folks might think you fond of me!

Refrain *Slow*
p-mf

I'll call 'round a - bout Three times a

day; May - be I could make it four!

You may throw me out Three times a

day, But I'll come right back for more!

When the sky falls in - to the

SWEET AND LOW-DOWN

Music and Lyrics by
GEORGE GERSHWIN
and IRA GERSHWIN

WHEN DO WE DANCE

Words By
IRA GERSHWIN

Music By
GEORGE GERSHWIN

LOOKING FOR A BOY

Music and Lyrics by
GEORGE GERSHWIN
and IRA GERSHWIN

KICKIN' THE CLOUDS AWAY

Words By
B.G. DeSYLVA and IRA GERSHWIN

Music By
GEORGE GERSHWIN

THAT CERTAIN FEELING

Music and Lyrics by
GEORGE GERSHWIN
and IRA GERSHWIN

THE SIGNAL

Words By
OTTO HARBACH and OSCAR HAMMERSTEIN II

Music By
GEORGE GERSHWIN

lov - er, dear, Give him a kiss for me. I can

hear a sound like some - one call - ing some - one, And I

won - der, dear, who can it be? The one whose voice I'm

hear- ing now, That one I feign would see!

Ped. ✱

SONG OF THE FLAME

Words By
OTTO HARBACH and OSCAR HAMMERSTEIN II

Music By
GEORGE GERSHWIN and HERBERT STOTHART

CLAP YO' HANDS

Music and Lyrics by
GEORGE GERSHWIN
and IRA GERSHWIN

MAYBE

Music and Lyrics by
GEORGE GERSHWIN
and IRA GERSHWIN

FIDGETY FEET

Music and Lyrics by
GEORGE GERSHWIN
and **IRA GERSHWIN**

Some-thing is the mat-ter with me Oh, but it's chron - ic!

Do you need a ton - ic? Oh! can't you see A

dumb thing is the mat-ter with me. I'm in con - di - tion,

OH, KAY

Words By
IRA GERSHWIN and HOWARD DIETZ

Music By
GEORGE GERSHWIN

200

DO, DO, DO

Music and Lyrics by
GEORGE GERSHWIN
and IRA GERSHWIN

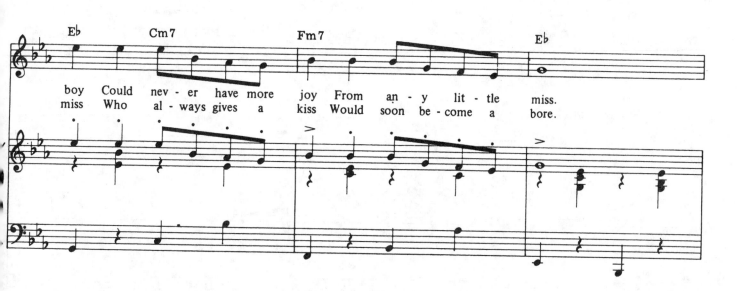

SOMEONE TO WATCH OVER ME

Music and Lyrics by
GEORGE GERSHWIN
and IRA GERSHWIN

206

HIGH HAT

Music and Lyrics by
GEORGE GERSHWIN
and **IRA GERSHWIN**

He: No use step-ping out that way, the thing to do is lay low;

you can't win by treat-ing her as if she wore a ha - lo.

Chorus: What is your so - lu - tion? Tell us if you can.

He: Here's my con - tri - bu - tion to man: High

LET'S KISS AND MAKE UP

Music and Lyrics by
GEORGE GERSHWIN
and IRA GERSHWIN

Jimmie: I did-n't mean to start an-y scene to make you sigh. Hope to die! — **Frankie:** It's most im-mor-al, For us to quar-rel; Why can't we Both a-

214

FUNNY FACE

Music and Lyrics by
GEORGE GERSHWIN
and IRA GERSHWIN

HE LOVES AND SHE LOVES

Music and Lyrics by
GEORGE GERSHWIN
and IRA GERSHWIN

MY ONE AND ONLY
(What Am I Gonna Do)

Music and Lyrics by
GEORGE GERSHWIN
and IRA GERSHWIN

'S WONDERFUL

Music and Lyrics by
GEORGE GERSHWIN
and IRA GERSHWIN

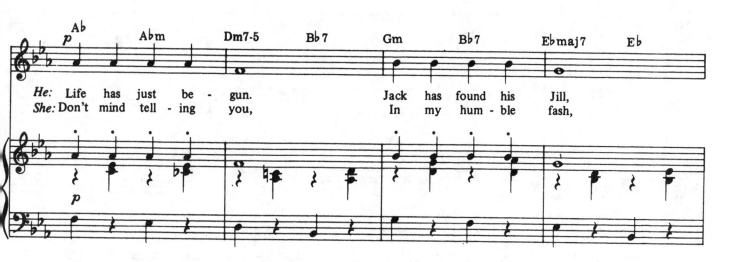

He: Life has just be - gun.   Jack has found his Jill,
She: Don't mind tell - ing you,   In my hum - ble fash,

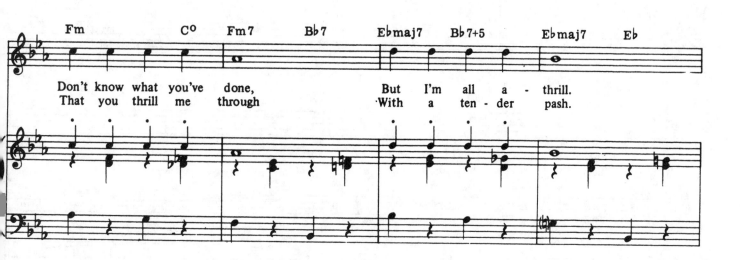

Don't know what you've done,   But I'm all a - thrill.
That you thrill me through   With a ten - der pash.

THE BABBITT AND THE BROMIDE

Music and Lyrics by
GEORGE GERSHWIN
and IRA GERSHWIN

234

They both were sol-id cit-i-zens they
That they had both de-vel-oped in ten
A harp each one was car-ry-ing and

both had been a-round, And as they spoke you clear-ly saw their
years, there was no doubt, And so, of course, they had an aw-ful
both were wear-ing wings, And this is what they said as they were

feet were on the ground.
lot to talk a-bout;
strum-ming on the strings;

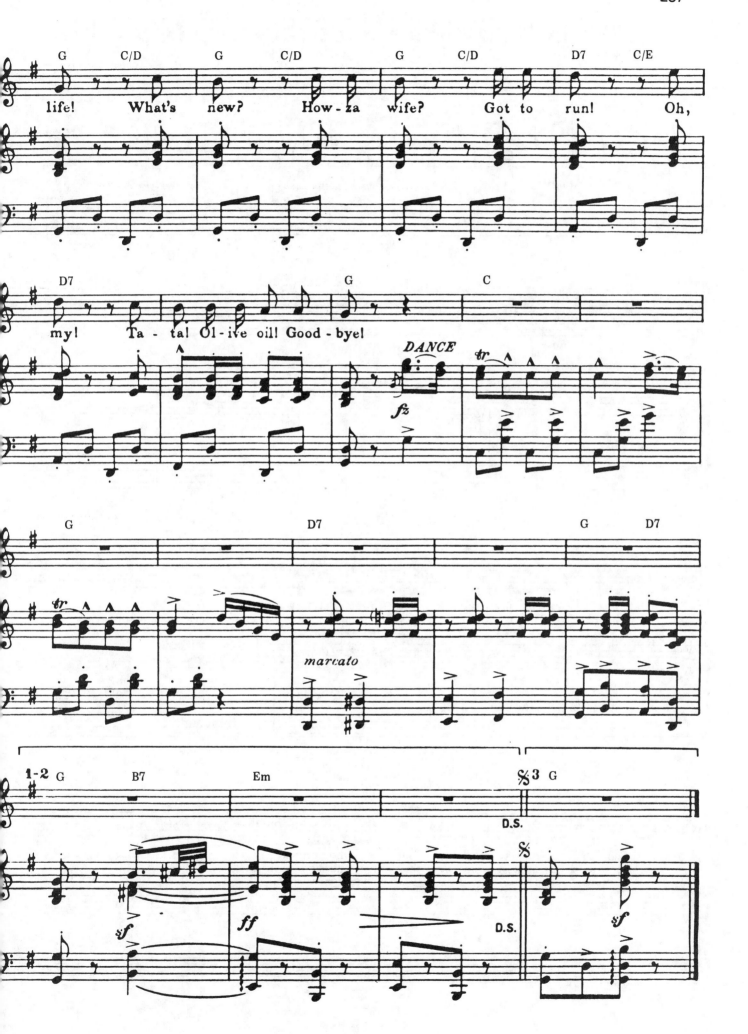

HOW LONG HAS THIS BEEN GOING ON?

Music and Lyrics by
GEORGE GERSHWIN
and IRA GERSHWIN

He: As a tot, when I trot-ted in lit-tle vel-vet pant ies,_____
She: 'Neath the stars at ba-zaars of-ten I've had to ca-ress men,_____

I was kissed by my sis-ters, my cous-ins and my aunt ies._____
Five or ten dol-lars then I'd col-lect from all those yes men._____

Sad to tell, it was Hell, an in-fer-no worse than Dan te's._____
Don't be sad, I must add that they meant no more than chess men._____

ROSALIE

Music and Lyrics by
GEORGE GERSHWIN
and IRA GERSHWIN

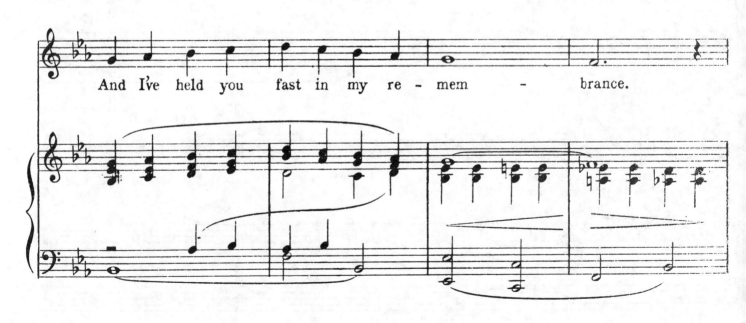

There's a vis - ion of you ev - er in my heart,———

Dear - er to me than a thous - and Rem - brandts.

I must tell you of the spell you cast when you're a - round,

Can not hide it, Must con'-fide it, Par - a - dise I've found.

*Open strings

K-RA-ZY FOR YOU

Music and Lyrics by
GEORGE GERSHWIN
and IRA GERSHWIN

Allegretto

Nat: When a guy like By - ron Would meet up with a si - ren,
Polly: Dar - ling, I have nev - er Heard such a grand en - deav - or,

In his dome He'd find a pome That made the girl - ie's skin burn.
Though your bent for sen - ti - ment Is not ex - act - ly to - ney.

I can-not spill pas - sion In high-fa - lu-tin' fash - ion;
Though you sing my prais - es In most pe - cul - iar phras - es,

I'm a - fraid that with a maid I'll nev - er be a Swin-burne. But,
Yet I see that they are free From what is called "bo - log - ney!" My

though I'm not the slight - est bit po - et - ic, ____
dear, your kind of po - et - ry will do me; ____

In my own way you will find me sym - pa - thet - ic.
'F a - ny - bod - y does - n't like it, let him sue me!

FEELING I'M FALLING

Music and Lyrics by
GEORGE GERSHWIN
and IRA GERSHWIN

felt it the mo-ment I found you. ———— This

felt it the mo-ment I found you. This

fail-ing I'm feel-ing keeps call-ing, dear, —— It's

fail-ing I'm feel-ing keeps call-ing, dear, —— It's

fa-tal, can't wait-'ll I'm 'round you. I'd like to

fa-tal, can't wait-'ll I'm 'round you. Oh, if you

tell you of the flame that makes me flut-ter, ————

feel you've found the one girl, please en-fold her, ————

mf espressivo

I DON'T THINK I'LL FALL IN LOVE TODAY

Music and Lyrics by
GEORGE GERSHWIN
and IRA GERSHWIN

I'VE GOT A CRUSH ON YOU

Music and Lyrics by
GEORGE GERSHWIN
and IRA GERSHWIN

Allegretto giocoso *(gaily)*

He: How
She: How

glad the man-y mil-lions of An-na-belles and Lill-ians would be
glad a mil-lion lad-dies from mill-ion-aires to cad-dies would be

— to cap-ture me! But you had such per-sist-ence, you

wore down my re-sist-ance: I fell, _____ and it was swell. _____

She: You're my big and brave and hand-some Ro-me-o. How I

won you I shall nev-er, nev-er know. *He:* It's not that you're at-trac-tive, But

260

LIZA
(All The Clouds'll Roll Away)

Music and Lyrics by
GEORGE GERSHWIN
and IRA GERSHWIN

EMBRACEABLE YOU

Music and Lyrics by
GEORGE GERSHWIN
and IRA GERSHWIN

What was it that con-trolled_ me? What kept my love-life lean?
My nose I used to turn _ up When you'd be-siege my heart;

My in-tu-i-tion told _ me You'd come on the scene. La-dy,
Now I com-plete-ly burn _ up When you're slow to start. I'm a-

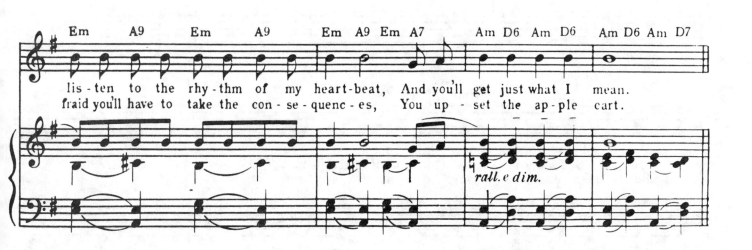

lis-ten to the rhy-thm of my heart-beat, And you'll get just what I mean.
fraid you'll have to take the con-se-quenc-es, You up-set the ap-ple cart.

MADEMOISELLE IN NEW ROCHELLE

Music and Lyrics by
GEORGE GERSHWIN
and IRA GERSHWIN

I GOT RHYTHM

Music and Lyrics by
GEORGE GERSHWIN
and IRA GERSHWIN

SAM AND DELILAH

Music and Lyrics by
GEORGE GERSHWIN
and IRA GERSHWIN

Tempo di Blues

De - li - lah ___ Was a flooz - y, _____

She nev - er ___ gave a damn; _____

De - li - lah —— was-n't choos-ey —————— Till she

fell For a swell buck-a - roo whose name was Sam. ——————

De - li - lah —— got in ac - tion, ——

—— De - li - lah —— did her

Lyrics:
His true wife ___ He did crave. ___ De - li - lah ___ She got jeal - ous, ___ And she tracked him and hacked him And dug for Sam a grave. ___

It's al-ways that way with pas-sion, So, cow-boy, learn to be-

have, Or else you're li-'ble to cash in

With no tomb-stone on your grave.

De-li-lah, Oh! De-li-lah,

MILITARY DANCING DRILL

Music and Lyrics by
GEORGE GERSHWIN
and **IRA GERSHWIN**

Ev-'ry moth-er's daugh-ter, If you're look-ing as you ough-ter, Will sur - ren - der.

Prop - er - ly done, Right from the start, Sol - dier, you've won, You've

cap - tured her heart, Do - ing the ver - y Gay, mil - i - tar - y

Danc-ing drill.

Danc-ing drill.

STRIKE UP THE BAND

Music and Lyrics by
GEORGE GERSHWIN
and IRA GERSHWIN

Refrain: *very marked*

Let the drums roll out! _____ Let the trum-pet call! _____ While the
(Boom boom boom!) (Ta-ta - ra - ta-ta-ta-ta!)

peo-ple shout! _____ Strike up the band! _____ Hear the cym-bals ring! _____
(Hoo - ray!)

_____ Call-ing one and all _____ To the mar-tial swing _____
(Tszing - tszing - tszing!) (Ta-ta - ra - ta-ta-ta-ta!) (Left,

_____ Strike up the band! _____ There is work to be done, to be
right!) Yan-kee Doo, Doo-dle-oo, Doo-dle-

SOON

Music and Lyrics by
GEORGE GERSHWIN
and IRA GERSHWIN

He: I'm mak - ing up for all the years that I wait - ed, I'm com - pen - sat - ed at last.

My heart is through with shirk - ing, thanks to you it's work - ing

BIDIN' MY TIME

Music and Lyrics by
GEORGE GERSHWIN
and IRA GERSHWIN

Moderato

Gracefully

Some fel-lers love to Tip-Toe Through The Tu-lips;
Some fel-lers love to Tell It To The Dai-sies;

Some fel-lers go on Sing - ing In The Rain.
Some Stroll Be-neath The Hon - ey-suc-kle Vines;

TREAT ME ROUGH

Music and Lyrics by
GEORGE GERSHWIN
and IRA GERSHWIN

When I was born they found a sil-ver spoon in my mouth;— I had a bar-ber just to curl my hair._____ If Win-ter came, the ma-ter car-ried me to the South;— The point is that I had the best of care._____ Wo-men and head-wait-ers fawned on me—

COULD YOU USE ME?

Music and Lyrics by
GEORGE GERSHWIN
and IRA GERSHWIN

Danny: Have some pit-y on an East-ern-er;
Ginger: There's a chap I know in Mex-i-co,

Show a lit-tle sym-pa-thy;
Who's as strong as he can be;

No one pos-si-bly could
Eat-ing nails and drink-ing

be stern-er
Tex-a-co

Than you have been with me.
He is the type for me.

There's a job that I'm ap-
There is one in Cal-i-

304

BUT NOT FOR ME

Music and Lyrics by
GEORGE GERSHWIN
and IRA GERSHWIN

Moderato

Old Man Sun - shine lis - ten, you! Nev - er tell me,

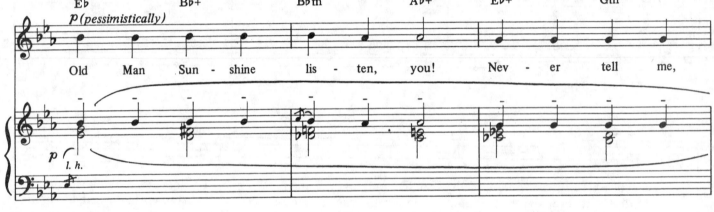

"Dreams come true!" Just try it And I'll start a ri - ot.

BOY! WHAT LOVE HAS DONE TO ME!

Music and Lyrics by
GEORGE GERSHWIN
and IRA GERSHWIN

REFRAIN

314

WINTERGREEN FOR PRESIDENT

Music and Lyrics by
GEORGE GERSHWIN
and IRA GERSHWIN

LOVE IS SWEEPING THE COUNTRY

Music and Lyrics by
GEORGE GERSHWIN
and IRA GERSHWIN

WHO CARES?
(So Long As You Care For Me)

Music and Lyrics by
GEORGE GERSHWIN
and IRA GERSHWIN

Let it rain and thun-der! Let a mil-lion

firms go un-der! I am not con-cerned with

Refrain

OF THEE I SING

Music and Lyrics by
GEORGE GERSHWIN
and IRA GERSHWIN

From the Is-land of Man-hat-tan to the Coast of Gold, From North to South, From East to West, You are the love I love the best.

BECAUSE, BECAUSE

Music and Lyrics by
GEORGE GERSHWIN
and **IRA GERSHWIN**

LORELEI

Music and Lyrics by
GEORGE GERSHWIN
and IRA GERSHWIN

MINE

Music and Lyrics by
GEORGE GERSHWIN
and IRA GERSHWIN

BLUE BLUE BLUE

Music and Lyrics by
GEORGE GERSHWIN
and IRA GERSHWIN

that's why we're paint-ing the White House blue!

rit.

Refrain: **Moderato** *(slowly, with expression)*

Blue, Blue, Blue! Not pink or pur-ple or yel-low, Not

brown like Mis-ter O - thel - lo, But Blue, Blue,

Blue! The coun-try clam-ored for some-bod- y new,— And grew e-

ISN'T IT A PITY

Music and Lyrics by
GEORGE GERSHWIN
and IRA GERSHWIN

LET 'EM EAT CAKE

Music and Lyrics by
GEORGE GERSHWIN
and IRA GERSHWIN

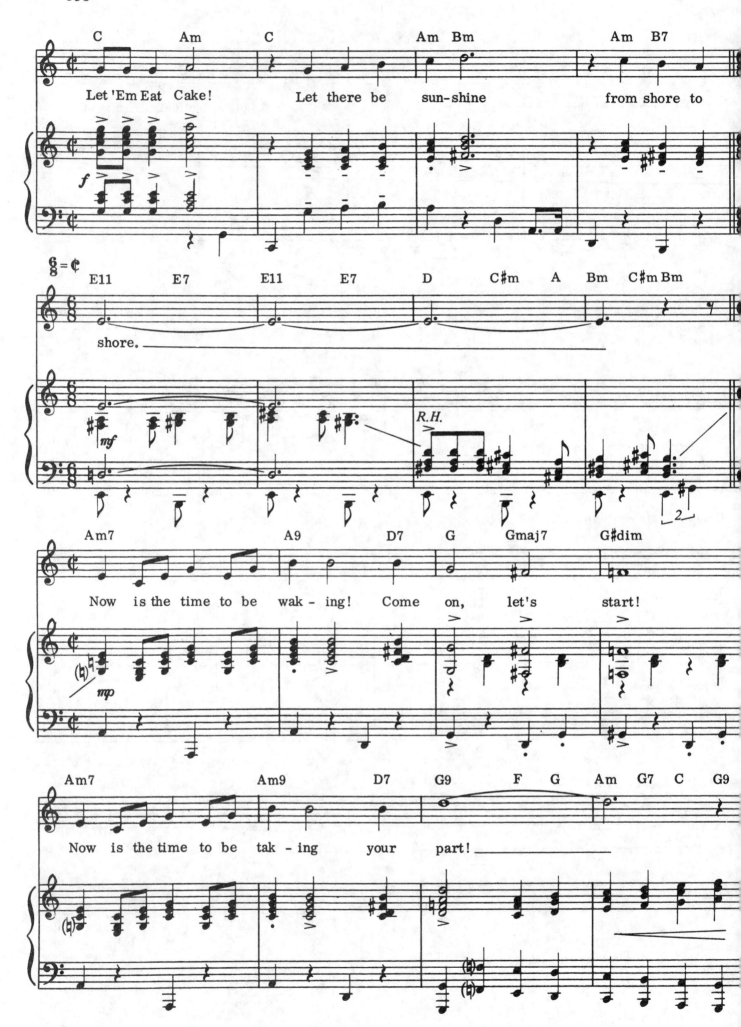

Let 'Em Eat Cake! Let there be sun-shine from shore to

shore. _____

Now is the time to be wak - ing! Come on, let's start!

Now is the time to be tak - ing your part! _____

MY COUSIN IN MILWAUKEE

Music and Lyrics by
GEORGE GERSHWIN
and IRA GERSHWIN

362

MISCHA, YASCHA, TOSCHA, SASCHA

Music and Lyrics by
GEORGE GERSHWIN
and ARTHUR FRANCIS

ain:

Temp-r'a- men - tal   O - ri - en - tal   Gen-tle-men   are   we,

Mis - cha Yas - cha,   Tos - cha Sas - cha,   Fid-dle le   fid-dle le   dee.

Shake-speare says."What's   in   a name?" With   him we   dis - a - gree.

We   give   cre - dit   when it's due, But   then you must   a - gree.
We're   not   high-brows,   we're not low-brows   An - y   one   can   see.

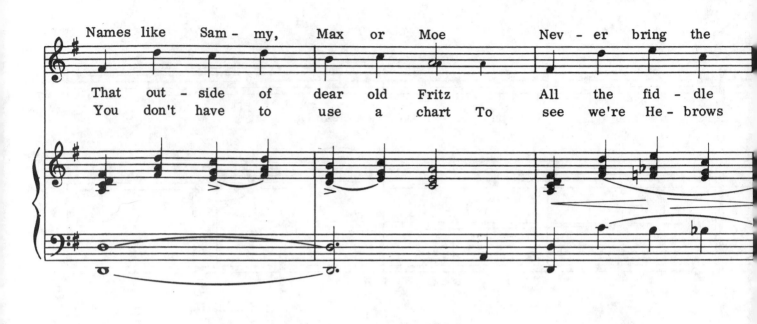

Names like Sam - my, Max or Moe Nev - er bring the

That out - side of dear old Fritz All the fid - dle

You don't have to use a chart To see we're He - brows

heav - y dough, Just

con - cert hits are } Mis - cha Yas - cha, Tos - cha Sas - cha,

from the start, Just

Fid-dle le fid-dle le dee. dee.